TALK! TALK! TALK!

A HAITIAN FABLE
RETOLD BY KAY WINTERS
ILLUSTRATED BY JOANN KITCHEL

Celebration Press
An Imprint of Pearson Learning

There once was a turtle who lived by a little pond in Haiti. He loved to sit in the sun and talk to all his friends who came to the pond for a drink. Talk! Talk! Talk!

Many of Turtle's friends were birds. One day the birds decided to leave Haiti. They wanted to take a trip to a faraway spot. "Let's go to New York," they said.

All of the birds began to chatter away about their long trip.

5

Soon Turtle's animal friends stopped
by the pond for a drink. Turtle talked to
them about the birds who were flying to
New York. He wanted so much to go on a
long trip. Talk! Talk! Talk!

Suddenly, a young pigeon flew down and sat on Turtle's log. He started to take a bath in the cool pond water.

"What is it like to fly?" asked Turtle.

"It's like riding on the wind," said Pigeon. "You can see so many wonderful places."

Turtle sighed. "Think of it," he said. "I have never been away from my little pond."

Pigeon felt sorry for Turtle.
"Why not come with me to New York?"
he said.

"What is it like in New York?" asked Turtle.

"The buildings are very tall," said Pigeon.
"There are crowds of people and rows of
cars. You could live in the big pond in
Central Park."

Turtle thought about moving to a new place. It was just what he wanted to do! But then, he looked down at his round shell and stumpy legs.

"How can I get to New York?" asked Turtle. "I have no wings to fly. I can only crawl."

And he looked sadly at his little pond.

Suddenly, Pigeon had an idea. "I know what we can do," he said. "I'll hold the end of a stick in my mouth. You hold the other end tightly in yours. But you must not say a word. Can you do that?"

"Of course, I can!" said Turtle. And he slipped off the log to share his news with all his friends. Talk! Talk! Talk!

15

There was work to be done. Pigeon and Turtle looked around the pond for a stick. They found a long one behind a tree. Pigeon took one end of the stick in his beak. Then he gave the other end to Turtle. Crunch! Turtle bit down hard to hold the stick in his mouth.

Up, up, up they flew over the little pond. Turtle wanted to shout down to all his animal friends, "Look at me! I'm flying!" But he didn't say a word.

As they flew close to the ocean, Turtle saw his animal friends waving on the shore. They were waving good-bye to all the birds flying to New York.

The animals began to laugh when they saw Turtle and Pigeon high in the sky. "Look up there! It's a flying turtle!" they shouted. "Even Turtle is flying to New York!"

Turtle was pleased to hear the animals talking about him. He called out as loud as he could, "Bye-bye!" And when Turtle opened his mouth, he let go of the stick. Down, down, down he fell into the ocean.

Pigeon couldn't stop to help Turtle. He needed to fly faster to catch up to the others. But with his soft, gray wings, he waved good-bye to Turtle.

And to this day, Turtle sits on a log in Haiti because he couldn't stop talking. Talk! Talk! TALK!